A Song in the Night

The Darker the Midnight,
The Brighter the Starlight

A Collection of Poems

Hildegard Bonacker Bruni

The EC Publishing LLC books may be ordered
through booksellers or by contacting:

EC Publishing LLC
116 South Magnolia Ave.
Suite 3, Unit F
Ocala, FL 34471, USA
Direct Line: +1 (352) 644-6538
Fax: +1 (800) 483-1813
http://www.ecpublishingllc.com/

Ordering Information:
Quantity sales. Special discounts are available on quan-
tity purchases by corporations, associations, and others.
For details, contact the publisher at the address above.

Printed in the United States of America

DEDICATION

I dedicate my poems to my husband, Dr. Aldo R. Bruni, MD,
And to my late sister, Emma Kirstein, for
whom I wrote my very first poems.
Both inspired me to write poetry.

But foremost, I dedicate my second
publication of my poems
To my mother, Emilie Bonacker.
She planted the seeds of nobility into my young heart.
Her simple Christian faith was hers, which
later became my moral foundation.

I want to express my gratitude to my friends, Dr. Kenneth
Maier, and Rebecca Egly, who were kind enough to take
time out of their busy schedules to edit my poems, and
I am grateful to my friend, Helga Kielnecker, for her help.

I would also like to thank all my family, relatives,
and friends, who were profoundly moved by some
poems inspired and delighted by others.
They encouraged me to publish them.

Henry Wadsworth Longfellow expresses in his poem, THE DAY IS DONE, which kind of poetry he likes to hear when sorrow and sadness overcome him:

Read from some humbler poet,
Whose songs gushed from the heart,
As showers from the cloud of summer,
And tears from the eyelids start;

Who, through long days of labor,
And nights devoid of ease,
Still heard in his soul the music
Of wonderful melodies.

Such songs have power to quiet
The restless pulse of care,
And come like a benediction
That follows after prayer.

Such humble yet thought-provoking poems wrote I, to glorify God, and bring inspiration, comfort, encouragement, and delight to the readers, who take the time to find something of their liking.

Hildegard Bonacker Bruni

Author

FOREWORD

This collection of poems, **A SONG IN THE NIGHT,** *The Darker the Midnight, The Brighter the Starlight,* had a humble beginning. In 1976 my husband, Dr. Aldo Bruni, and I celebrated our tenth wedding anniversary. What better gift could I give him than poems written about the ten years shared and the loveliness of nature?

Also, in 1976, the United States of America celebrated the Bicentennial. I wanted to contribute to my adopted country and express my gratitude and admiration for the history and beauty of North America in my poems.

But how do I begin writing poetry when I have never done it? I asked my nephew, Bernhad Kirstein, who had studied journalism if he could recommend a book on how to write poetry. He gave me: *Sound and Sense*, an introduction to Poetry, by Lawrence Perrine.

As I read the instructions, I wrote my first poem Ten years ago. With each new poem, the meter flowed better. The more I wrote, the more I enjoyed expressing thoughts and emotions in poetic, rhythmic verses.

On April 2, 1976, the day of our 10th Wedding Anniversary, I presented my first hand-written collection of poems called: **"For Aldo"** to my husband. He enjoyed them very much and asked me when I had written all these poems. He was amazed when I told him I had written them at night.

Wanting to refine my newly acquired hobby, I enrolled in a course in Creative Writing at Harper College in Palatine, Illinois.

I continued writing poetry. I was delighted to see some published by The International Society of Poetry. They chose me as Poet of the Year in 2000.

The second motif prompting me to choose the title of my book was the fortitude of the people who survived the terrorist attack in New York on September 11, 2002, and persons who lost their loved ones. I respect the courageous firefighters and rescue workers who rushed to the scene, risking their lives to help the survivors. They buried their pain and grief in faith, comfort, and patriotic songs. I express my thoughts and emotions about this tragedy in the poem: A DAY TO REMEMBER.

The third reason I elected the title: "A SONG IN THE NIGHT" is to remember the horrors of WWII, when hunger and constant danger surrounded us, and life became extremely trying, yet we still sang a song of praise to God. Through His mercy and protection, our lives were spared.

Recalling the past gave birth to my poem: **Escape from East Prussia**, where my four brothers, three sisters, and I were born. During the Second World War, we, and people from all countries involved in WWII, went through so much hardship. Mothers and children like us and millions of refugees who lost their homes endured indescribable suffering to escape torture and death from the Russian Army. They, too, kept a song in their hearts and faith in God, even in the darkest of nights.

During our escape on horse and wagon from East Prussia in 1944-1945, my mother, Emilie Bonacker, 46, and my three sisters, Emma, twenty; Marta, eighteen; and Meta, sixteen, were such heroic women. I have the highest respect for them. They gave their already scarce food to the younger brother, Horst, who was one and a half years old, and me, seven. They walked in the snow for miles and miles to ease the load of the horses. They dug for food, begged, and gathered anything eatable so we would not starve. They took us to shelters during air raids. They milked cows at the farms where we stayed so we would get food in return. Marta helped care for wounded soldiers in a hospital.

My older brothers, Georg, thirteen; Edmund, twelve; and Richard, nine, aged prematurely. They had to do men's work during the eight months of journey by horse and wagon. They took care of the horses, begged for fodder, and helped in any possible way so that we would stay alive. It is a miracle we all survived with the help of six other mothers, two soldiers, and two fathers; however, it was primarily because of God's protection. To this date, I am grateful to God and all who have helped us.

My sister Marta fled with the teacher's family, got separated from them, and ended up in Silkerode, which later became the five-kilometer-wide demilitarized zone under the Russian occupation. She met her husband there and raised her three children surrounded by Russian guards under challenging conditions. After one year of searching through the Red Cross and relatives, we found each other.

God wiped away all tears of sorrow from mother, father, sisters Emma, Marta, Meta, and brothers Georg and Richard and gave them eternal joy. They have already gone to their heavenly home, where no more suffering will occur.

Briefly, I shall attempt to explain the conditions in Germany after WWII ended. The Allies divided Germany into four zones. The American Army occupied the Southern part of Germany. The British occupied the Northern section, the French the South Western portion, and the Russian Army the Eastern region. The northern part of East Prussia was given according to the Potsdam Treaty to the Russian

Government, and the southern part was given to Poland. With the consent of the three Allies, the Russian Government gave Pomerania and Selesia as restitution for a section the Russians had taken from Poland. Yugoslavia demanded a portion of the South Eastern part of Germany. Thus, Germany lost one-third of its territory, the agricultural section.

The German inhabitants who remained in these Eastern provinces were stripped of their rights, chased from their property, humiliated, beaten, or, if capable of working, kept as forced laborers under the most inhumane conditions. If they resisted, they were shot on the spot. Even their own people suffered severe punishments for helping any Germans. Despite these circumstances, many merciful people shared their little food with the less fortunate. Not until much later did the American and British Governments learn of the atrocious conditions, making the mass evacuation more tolerable. Thousands upon thousands died from hunger, disease, and heavy work or were shot or tortured to death in the most un-imaginable ways. It is hard to believe that Man's inhumanity to Men had reached a new low. The revenge and hate for our dictator and his cruelties were taken out on the innocent German citizens.

The fortunate ones who escaped to West Germany also found poor housing and food conditions there. Bombs had destroyed forty percent of all homes and apartments, and little food was left to share.

We lived with fourteen people in a one-bedroom apartment on a huge farm for some time. We were grateful to have a roof over our heads and to receive milk and food. In exchange, my brother Georg worked in the fields, and sisters Emma and Meta milked cows for meager pay and food rations.

In June 1947, the United States established the Marshall Plan to help the European Nations rebuild their countries. Even though Germany received the smallest amount per capita, the German Government and their ambitious, resourceful, and hardworking men and women rebuilt Germany rapidly. Germany became once more the vital industrial nation in Europe.

Many refugees immigrated to the United States, Canada, and other parts of the world. They contributed to the countries that gave them a new home. My brother Edmund, my sisters Emma and Meta, and I in 1956, chose the United States of America as our permanent home, and we all became American citizens.

I am very grateful to all the people in America who sent CARE packages with food and clothing immediately after the war. I express gratitude to the American Government, who assisted Germany through the Marshall Plan to rebuild the shattered remnant of the country, and to all the courageous, capable, fortunate German men and women who survived the horrors of WWII.

I want to pay a special tribute to the women who went and still go through heartbreaking experiences, whether it is war, political oppression, injustice, work-related problems, poverty, abuse, emotional or physical sickness, family problems, taking care of handicapped or terminally ill loved ones, aged parents, or deal with the daily stress of modern, fast-paced life, and still keep a song in their hearts. These heroic women are seldom decorated or remembered. No monuments are erected in their honor.

I revere you and say: Keep singing and looking up under any circumstances.

Earthly troubles are short-lived. Life is a precious gift from God, and what we make of life is our gift to God. Together with the Master Weaver, using our joys, sorrows, and experiences as threads, we can create a beautiful work of art. We always have to nurture a vision, a dream, or a goal; otherwise, we will perish.

This collection of poems is a gift to you, my dear readers, relatives, and wonderful friends worldwide. I would like to share a broad palette of human emotions and God's wonders and beauty of life and nature.

My greatest wish, however, is that wars would become obsolete and we would learn to settle our differences through diplomacy without seeking each other's death. Then, we could live together with dignity and peace as caring global brothers, sharing our goods and resources with the less fortunate.

I would like to honor and commemorate the heroic women of WWII from Europe, the United States, Russia, Japan, and all countries involved who sacrificed so much for their families and their countries and whose courage, love, faith, patience, and hard work healed the war-torn wounds, with a monument, proceeds from the sale of this book, permitting.

I would call this memorial:

HEROINES OF WWII

Hildegard Bonacker Bruni

Author

A SONG IN THE NIGHT

When I'm surrounded by darkness, all

Stars are stripped from my velvet sky;

There burns a flame within my soul

That shines day and night. I glorify

With songs of praise my awesome God,

Who eases crushing loads of woe.

He fills with joy and peace my heart

To face triumphantly each foe.

Sunshine returns like a balm after rain.

A calm follows behind each squall.

For deeper grow the roots of mine,

And higher ascends my stronger soul.

PATRIOTISM

ODE TO THE AMERICAN FLAG

Among the youngest in the world
You are, with love and honor upheld.
You stand for freedom, justice, peace.
And orbit proudly in outer-space.

You landed on the moon, and so
Reached uncharted frontiers. You glow
At night by moon- and starlight and send
Peace and goodwill to all mankind.

You witnessed America's finest hour;
But flew in shame and sadness lower,
When assassins killed Presidents,
Or their lives would naturally end.

You cheered soldiers in battlefields,
Embraced the coffins when broken their shields.
Where victory won, you proudly stood,
To foe and the world, your power showed.

You mark each American institution.
We display you with deep devotion
In our country and oversea.
Fly forever in the land of the free.

SCENIC BEAUTY OF AMERICA

I traveled to many countries of the world.
Saw all the different States of our Union:
But none do I hold dearer to my heart
Than North America. In my opinion,
It is God's crowning masterpiece of beauty.

We'll take with the sun across our land a journey,
Observe, by spring-enhanced, her changing beauty:
She rises over the Atlantic with splendid displays
Along the shore of ancient granite cliffs,
Which turns the waves into fountain sprays.

She climbs and pauses on top of the rugged bluffs,
Where sapphire lakes are anxious to reflect
Forest bedecked hills, a cloud-speckled sky.
Trees and plants to her kiss and warmth react.
They blush to brilliant blossoms, gently and shy.

She hurries to the endless Southern shore,
Begs birds and bathers to crowd sandy beaches,
Waves and palms, their ceaseless concert roar
Before she a magnificent wide river bed reaches,
She casts giant shadows among towering ridges

And on wild flower tufted mountain meadows,
Which flaunt their vast pastoral loveliness.
She rides the rapids of the mighty river,
Then meanders and makes many bends
To carry soil from the fertile, rich heartlands,

And forest songs from the deep dark Northwoods,
Which are adorned with glacial lakes by the thousands.
She mounts the clouds above the fertile fields
And spans a rainbow over the vast prairie.
Where once like swaying ships under full sail,

The prairie schooners their pioneers did carry.
She burns the Southern plains into a desert,
Creates weird parks of bushes and giant cacti.
Some blooming brightly, others old and withered
Pointing like giant sentinels to the sky.

Weary of the boundless fields and prairies
She ascends the rugged mountain chains.
Every turn reveals a new surprise.
Lakes are set as prettily as gems
In valleys among covered granite cliffs,

Still showing pockets filled with snow and ice.
Streams are churning through the rocky canyons
Forming foaming cascades that do thunder
Down the steep and massive pinnacles.
She enters a world of surprise and wonder,

Among bubbling mud, erupting tall geysers.
Amid the Cascades, she breathlessly gazes
Into a deep, blue Crater Lake.
She plays in the grandeur of canyon scapes,
Leaps over hot, arid, yet blooming deserts.

Then, through an arcade of tall redwood slithers,
Which stretch the sky with their ancient treetops.
She basks in the Pacific Ocean. At eventide,
Dresses in pink like a young, blushing bride.
She kisses "Good Night" the alluring shore.

The waves and the wind her evening attire adore.
She dreams of a land where ice runs in deep rivers.
And a sea of antlers through the tundra thunders.
She pictures fair maidens waiting on tropical isles
To greet her with flowers and hearts full of smiles.

Many places in the world, I saw
But none find I lovelier than America.

A DAY TO REMEMBER

The eleventh of September
Is a day we always will remember.
We wrote the year Two-Thousand-One,
When terrorists attacked New York that morn.

They flew a highjacked plane and smashed
One tower of the World Trade Center. Glass crashed,
Flames melted steel. The concrete crumbled
And buried men alive. Some stumbled

While running down the smoke-filled stairs.
Firefighters rushed to the tower with hoses and gears.
Heroic efforts at once began
To save as many lives as they possibly can.

Later, a plane hit the second tower.
The breath of fire, the dust of death devour
More innocent people, the landmark tall
Turns to ashes as the structures fall.

They explode and collapse,
After minutes elapse.
Smoke, ashes, debris
Fill part of the city.
People cry!
Thousands die.
Sirens scream.
The rescue team
Digs through debris
The injured to free.

Trucks rushed to clean
A path to the scene.
Red lights flash
Through smoke and ash.
Manhattan, oh horror,
Is wounded by terror.

The mayor rushes to ground zero.
To asses the damage, praise each courageous hero.
He tells New Yorkers they're not alone,
The world shares your grief of love ones, injured and gone.

While rescue work is going on
A third plane slams into the Pentagon.
A fourth crashed in an open field.
Pilots and passengers didn't to the highjackers yield.

They kept pretty low the intended death toll,
And gave their lives to save the capitol.
New flights are canceled. All planes must land
To prevent more disasters, the terrorists might have planned.

As the news worldwide breaks,
President Bush to Nations speaks:
"We'll bring to justice the guilty and say
To those who harbor the faceless enemy,

You'll get your punishment,
Unless you cooperate with our Government.
We must be resilient and fight mercilessly
To retore freedom from fear and security.

We must combat this tyranny,
Until we win the final victory,"
Worldwide and National pray'r vigils began

For the deceased, the injured, and for peace to remain.

"God Bless America" the Congress
Senate and People sang midst flag displays.
Patriotism blossomed everywhere.
So did compassion, courage, faith, and some fear.

Help poured in from all over exceedingly,
To rebuild lives, New York, and the economy.
God, through our faith, will heal this painful scar
And turn the dust of death into a flaming star.

Written in memory of those who lost their lives in the terrorist attack on September 11, 2001, and dedicated to President George W. Bush, New York Mayor Rudolph Giuliani, and all the courageous rescue workers, volunteers, helpful citizens of America, and compassionate people around the world.

LETTER OF PRESIDENT GEORGE W. BUSH

THE WHITE HOUSE

Thank you for writing about the acts of war committed against the United States on September 11 and for sending your thoughtful remembrance. In the face of this evil, our country remains strong and united, a beacon of freedom and opportunity to the rest of the world.

Our Government continues to function without interruption. Our intelligence, military, and law enforcement communities are working non-stop to find those responsible for these attacks. We will make no distinction between the terrorists who committed these acts and those who help or harbor them.

We must remember that our Arab and Muslim American citizens love our nation and must be treated with dignity and respect. Americans of every creed, ethnicity, and national origin must unite against our common enemies.

Since these terrible tragedies occurred, our citizens have been generous, kind, resourceful, and brave. I encourage all Americans to find a way to help. Websites like LibertyUnites.

org can serve as a resource for those wanting to participate in the relief efforts.

God bless you and your family, and God bless America.

BIRTH OF OUR NATION

America was ruled
By monarchies for years,
Whose laws and tyranny
Spread suffering and despair.

A strong voice cried
In every anguished heart:
"Let me be free! Let me be free!"
Leaders heard this urgent plea,

And organized all men,
Willing to die for liberty,
To defend their country
And their families.

They fought long, bloody wars
Courageously until
They won against all odds
And great adversity.

At last, they raised their flag
Of stars and stripes.
Victory theirs!
A Nation was born.

GEORGE WASHINGTON

If you think back on American history,
Who was the most influential of all men
To create a new Nation? It was George Washington.
He rose to gallant honor through integrity.

As General of a small and wavering army
He fought skilled soldiers of Britain's monarchy
Though victory seemed almost impossible,
He did not quit till his enemy weakened and fell.

When he was a statesman, again, he chose
A demanding path to serve his fellow men.
He urged all States to create one Union.
He succeeded despite many foes,

As first President, he set a fine example.
In God we trust, he chose as his preamble.
He placed his problems on his Master's Altar
God's wisdom helped him not to falter.

ABRAHAM LINCOLN

Who of all Presidents
Hold we dearest to our hearts?
If not Abraham Lincoln?
His quiet dignity lives on.

His long path to the White House
Was paved with endless failures.
His humble background didn't cause
Him to give up his dreams and goals.

He humbly set out to serve God,
His fellow man, his country.
He challenged opportunity
By doing what was right and good.

His most vital moral guideline was:
"Right makes might."
Here I stand; I can't do otherwise.
Never shall I compromise!"

WRITING OF THE CONSTITUTION

(Written in a trialogue between people, delegates, and God)

PEOPLE: "Yes, we are free from foreign legislation;
But look, what's happening to our nation?
Chaos reigns because we do not know,
Who will guide and unify us now?"

DELEGATES: "People are restless. Confusion is their master.
We must act quickly to prevent disaster.
Let us convene in Philadelphia,
And set up guidelines for a common law.

PEOPLE: We look to you with anxious expectation,
Only your wisdom can now save our nation.
You must embrace the interests of us all;
When you write the constitution as your rule.

DELEGATES: "We humbly bow in prayer: "Do not forsake
Us. We have great tasks to undertake.
Teach us Thy wisdom, Great Creator."

GOD: "Trust Me, and my divine wisdom.
Build in goodness, truth, and beauty my kingdom
Here on Earth. Obey and follow my ways,
And I will bless your people with eternal grace,
Exalt you as a model to all Nations.
If not, you'll suffer devastation".

DELEGATES: "Each person must be treated as an equal,
Retain the right to worship his own creed.
We'll balance power of States and Union well.
Too little Government anarchy breeds.
Too much depresses the people and degrades.
We, the Statesmen, must serve in honesty
Be elected by the people a certain way.
God bless and guide us so we may succeed.
Be patient, and forgive us if we erred."

PEOPLE: "The delegates show wisdom, are concerned
With our well-being, by making us the Government.
Now, it is up to each one of us to be
An honest, loyal citizen who is free
To help create a lasting democracy.
Let **IN GOD WE TRUST**, our preamble be".

SPACE FLIGHT DREAM

The countdown was zero. With a burning blast
The rocket took off from the launching mast.
Like a flaming arrow, it pierced the air,
Then left behind the global atmosphere.

I began to orbit past Earth's gravity
Viewed infinite wonders of cosmic majesty.
Up till now, no mortal has been able
To see the fragile earth like a white-blue marble

Floating through the magnificence of the universe.
The silver moon spun around and around the earth.
Like diamond dust, the stars studded the skies.
At times, the sun glowed like a ruby in my eyes.

The breathless splendor of the endless outer space
Imparted to me harmony and cosmic peace.
I joined the heavens to declare God's infinite glory
By reading to men from the Bible creation's great story.

When I returned to planet Earth again
I was a wiser, visionary woman.
I want to help mankind; I toil and strive
To improve on Earth the quality of life.

GRAND CANYON LAND

Did you ever see the canyon lands?
A giant rock garden, where Nature's Artists
Are chiseling out of colored rocks and sands
Imposing sculptors. You are so impressed,

You feel you stand on God's holy ground.
Listen, you will hear the awesome sound
Of river and wind still carving rock formations.
They're never content with their creations.

They work fast in the early morning glow.
At noon, they temper their work with rain and heat
At eventide, they let exquisitely flow
A golden sunset around their giant feet.

At night, the moon and stars do rise and ask:
"Why don't you rest and enjoy your task?"
They drowsily tarry for just a few moments,
Then, carve more majestic monuments.

NATURE

DAWNING OF A NEW DAY

Shyly, at dawn, the sun ascends behind the rugged mountain
tops,
And golden rays glide over the glistening surface of the sea.
 They rest on the sandy shore before they tiptoe through
the land.
Sunlight touches trees and flowers with a gentle kiss,
Then penetrates through windows to awaken sleepy
residents.
Soon, the sun appears in all its dazzling splendor
To celebrate the dawning of a newborn day.
 By driving the darkness of the night away,
 Light puts God's boundless wonders on display.

MORNING

Morning is a blessed time to meet with God
To meditate and pray for strength to face my lot.
God calms my spirit and lifts it to the mountaintop.
He fills my heart with joy and peace as I look up.

God buries troubles and fatigue each night.
He gives daily new energy that is just right
To fulfill my duties and stay calm and strong
Anchored firmly in God's love all day long.

I use my cross as a staff to help me carry on
And not as a stumbling block to cast me down.
When I carry my cross with dignity and a smile,

I may help others from sadness to gladness beguile,

I meet with God at the dawning of each day,
To read His precious word, meditate, and pray
For others and me, that I may grow in grace
Until He calls me home to meet Him face to face.

NIGHT

The evening crowned the night with golden clouds,
Removed the sunlight from her fading shrouds.
Night entered from the universe
To drop her veil of darkness over Earth.

Her countless eyes lit up the velvet sky
And gazed into the human heart to try
Deleting problems from each restless soul,
Then fill it with her peace so plentiful.

The song of the night rang like a whisper
Replaced with joy what seemed sinister.
Before her tender fingers closed my eyes,
And to the magic dreamland, I did rise,

I pondered, and I prayed; God may
Protect and bless my loved ones night and day.
I offered thanks for all the blessings I received,
And daily goals I gladly had achieved.

FROZEN BEAUTY

While darkness rests our tired eyes,
Nature creates a fairyland of ice.

Bushes branches crystallize
By the touch of her cold hand.

She guards her fragile masterpiece.
In the softest cloaks of clouds

Till everyone the beauty sees
She lavishly unfolds.

Then rushes on the wings of the wind
More precious work of art to send.

THE PONDEROSA TREE

Oh, Ponderosa tree,
You are so much like me:
Some branches are full of life and green,
Yet others, gnarled and dry, reach up to heaven.

You harbor many birds
In holes dug out in time,
And soak up warmth from the autumn sky.
When laden with snow you bend, in storms and sway;

But never break, just shake.
Each year, you grow new roots
To feed and reinforce your trunk;
Until the reaper comes and cuts you down.

COME OUTDOORS

Winds are whistling at my window,
Begging me to come outdoors:
"Look, explore the gifts of nature
And pick violets and daisies,
In the woods and open fields.
I'll renew your joy of living
Through a rendezvous with spring."

CHANGING SEASONS AT YOSEMITE

Half Dome, a temple in the air,
Stands draped in snow. The park is hushed,
And silence speaks. The river un-rushed,
Reflects the clouds and trees, now bare.

White waters wash the snow away.
Echoes of spring roar through the valley.
Black oaks unfurl their leaf display,
And dogwood blossoms flaunt their beauty.

The sun begins the summer race,
And paints against the northern sky
Silhouettes of peaks and trees,
And flowers in the meadows high.

As days drop, like the autumn leaves,
Fall flames in brilliant shades
Of red and gold. Away he fades,
And winter wanders down the cliffs.

A NEW DAY

I go to the tower
To greet a new day.

Two stars linger in the dawning sky.
Around the rocks, the waves still sleep.
A heron wades on the sandy shore
To feed on fish, some crabs, and more.

Above the surface of the calm sea
The pelicans undulate very low.
Finches cheerfully twitter in the tree
While in flight catches insects a swallow.

The droning of the boats
Breaks the sacred silence.
To the sea fishermen haste
To fill with fish their chests.

The sun spins veils of light.
Over the water and cliffs,
The morning star fades
And the rocks blush.

The sunrays glide on a golden carpet
 Over land and sea to town. They greet
And embrace me in her array,
And herald the dawning of a new day.

I fold my hands in reverence,
And reflect on God's benevolence.
I thank my MAKER for light and life,
All creatures on land, in the air, and the sea,

The beauty I see,
His love and glee.

DUSK IN SPRING

Dusk drapes the meadow slowly.
It's time to end the daily work.

Air balloons are gliding along,
And vanish in the twilight sky.

I listen to the meadowlark,
And twitter of a robin's song.

The breeze stokes gently the tender
Green branches, lulling them to rest.

The sun descends slowly in splendor
Bathing the earth in a mellow mist.

Before she is swallowed by darkness deep.
Creation is tenderly cradled to sleep.

My heart is filled with awe and praise;
For God revealed His masterpiece

The twilight of a radiant spring day
With all its loveliness in May.

THUNDER

The thunder beats in the distance a drum,
And raindrops dance to the thunder's tune.

Faster and faster goes his nearing beat,
And louder and louder grows the rumble.

In a raging frenzy, the drum burst,
And sparks of fire zigzag through the sky.

RAINDROPS

Like fine dotted silver threads,
Raindrops are falling from the sky.
Filling the empty riverbeds
To quench the thirst of lands so dry.

Born in oceans and seas,
Carried by the soaring breeze,
They embrace the flowers and trees,
And kiss the bloom of a blushing rose.

OUR FALCON PEDRO

While building our winter home.
A worker brought a wounded falcon.
We named him Pedro, adopted him,
To make him well was our aim.
We fixed his foot and injured wing,
Then tied him to a leather string.
He healed quickly and recovered well.
One day, he tried to fly but fell
Down to the ground. Now, he was free.
He walked away and looked at me,
Then stretched his wings and flew away.
Now Pedro set out to survey,
The beautiful sky, the home of his heart.
With mixed emotions, I saw him depart.
I waved to Pedro as he left home.
Then, later, I lost sight of him.

Each day, I went outside to check,
If he'd remember, how to come back.
One day, a shadow caught my eye
A bird perched on the tree nearby.
I dashed outside; I looked in awe,
It was Pedro who left months ago.
"Pedro!" I shouted up the tree
"I'm glad you have returned to me."
I talked to him. He turned his head
As if he knew just what I said.
Then, spread his wings, he began to fly
Away into the vaulted sky.

I'm happy now; he's well to spend,
Life in his element.

He plays with sun rays on his wings,
And hears when crashing thunder rings.
He watches lightning flashing by
Then glides with the wind soaring on high.
He has returned for thirty years,
And filled our hearts with endless cheers.
As each year passes, I have a concern,
Is he alive? Will he return?
I marvel at his faithfulness,
And how he shows his gratefulness.
We, too, are thankful and quite fond
Of our profound, lasting bond.
Pedro brought us endless pleasure.
He is God's gift, our priceless treasure.

THE SEA AND I

I play with sunrays on my limbs,
As a school of fish around me swims.
I catch a seaweed in my hand
And take it to the lonely strand.
I share its beauty with the sky.
Yet alone are we, the sea and I.

Surrounded just by sea and sand,
And rugged mountains, islands, land.
No house nor hut has found a place,
In our unspoiled paradise.
Just here and there, a plane darts by.
Yet alone are we, the sea and I.

I scan the sand of the shallow shore,
And search for driftwood, shells, and more.
I watch the ever-changing tides,
The sun behind a tall hill hides.
The stars fill up the empty sky.
Yet alone are we, the sea and I.

Oh sea, how well I understand,
We write our songs on the sand.
Yet hills will echo, eyes will see,
What we're composing, you and me,
I'll join your greater harmony
To sing forever, I and the Sea.

SAILING

Winds blow.
Restless are the rolled-up sails.

Waves grow.
Even the rudder begs direction.

Captains go
To sea with great anticipation.

RAGING LAKE MICHIGAN

Wild winds whip up waves in a fury.
The lake foams responds in a rage.
Waves trample on shore and bury
It under their liquid load. Then rush
Back and forth in roaring thunder,
Yet, they create a springtime wonder
Of rainbow-painted geysers in the sky.

A WET NOVEMBER DAY

Bare trees bow branches in their grief
And mourn the loss of every leaf.
Tears roll down the firmament,
While birds sing softly their lament.

WINTER WINDS

Winter winds
Sigh among the naked shoots
Lonely as lances.
While roots design
The blooming wonders
For the barren branches.

UNTAMED TEMPER

Tension mounts!
Smoke fills the air.
Suddenly, the volcano explodes,
And displays a violent eruption.
Down the mountain flow
Fire and lava, aglow,
Causing great destruction.

ALONE BY THE SEA

I went alone
Across the hill
To find some solitude
And cool off in the sea.
I lingered long among the waves
And let the wind caress my hair.

The sun rays kissed my skin.
I gently closed my eyes,
And dreamed of you.
For you're my sunshine,
Wind and Sea.

MOUNTAINS

Have you ever stopped and pondered why
God created mountains so massive and high.

Have you ever looked at a snowcapped peak
Without being strengthened when you felt weak?

God wants to lift our eyes heavenwards,
And free us from the worries of this earth.

GOD'S SPLENDOR

Could I describe
With the most eloquent words
The majesty of God's creation,
I would not even touch
The tiniest fragment of His splendor.

BEAUTY IN THE CLOUDS

Above the dense gray shrouds
There hides much beauty in the clouds.

Though they look dark viewed from below,
Their summit always is aglow.

I see in clouds from outer space
The dawning of the universe.

By morn they blush at the sun rays sight
And bathe themselves in warm daylight.

They bring new life to the barren lands,
And cool the farmer's toil-worn hands.

When chores complete, in the lower sphere,
They braid a rainbow in their hair.

Then pass on with the cleansing wind.
Their changing splendor has no end.

Though heavy hang the clouds of sorrow,
They seldom last beyond tomorrow.

After the veil of darkness lifts,
They reveal to me God's precious gifts.

STREAMS

Up on the hills among bare rocks
Two streams begin their separate paths.

At times, their waters join in lakes,
Just long enough to hold and share

The beauty of the sky and earth.
And then they go their separate ways,

Cleansed and enriched with joy again,
Doing what life demands of them.

Until one day, they reach their final goals
And join the ocean with all other streams.

DAWN

As the night says hello to the dawning day
The sky reveals faint mountain contours,
And clouds reflect their purple tints.
Pelican ribbons undulate

Over the surface of the sea.
Seagulls greet the dawning day,
With shrieks and lonely cries in the sky.
From the safety of the harbor

Shrimp boats head out to the sea.
Against the glowing horizon
The silhouette of the isle turns darker.
Behind the bluffs, the sun ascends,

Casting light across the bay.
The magic of dawn radiantly
Gives birth to a new spring day
In the beautiful month of May.

THE PELICAN SHOW

The Pelicans put on a show.
In unison, they flew to survey
The surface of the moving sea.
Then, one by one propelled himself,
Before diving into the water.
Rewarded by a fish in their beaks
They rode the undulating waves.
When a fishing boat crossed their paths
They mounted the updraft and circled the isle.
Cutting through sun rays in their flight.
Their wings reflected the morning light.
The day proceeded, and so did the birds,

THE FOG

Dense fog cloaks mountains, sea, and land,
Tries holding back the sunrays sent.

Yet soon, the sun appears in its glory,
And wipes away the fog in a hurry.

Dew drops dissolve, on the breeze ascend,
Then, cleanse the air and dust laden plant.

And so is my tribulation,
It serves my soul's purification.

So I may see God's endless beauty
And taste his love and tender mercy.

I leave the dust and fog behind,
And keep the pure and noble in mind.

MORNING DEW

A summer night turned unexpectedly cool!
At dawn, the dew drops hung on blades of grass.
As soon as the sun rays reached the transparent pearls,
They glistened and reflected all the rainbow colors.
Then gave birth to millions of tiny water droplets,
Who rose on the sun-beams up into the blue sky
To meet their companions in a gray, dense cloud.

QUIET MOMENTS

Oh, how I love that quiet time!
I watch the sunrays blink and bounce
Upon the wavelets of the sea.
I hear the rustle of the breeze
Combing through the tropical trees;
I gaze at a bougainvillea limb
On a rugged stone wall climb.

Oh, how I love that quiet time!
I listen to the songs of praise,
Composed by finches just for me.
I catch a glimpse of hummingbirds
Fighting playfully in flight.
An oriole clings to a blossom
Of an orange tulip tree.

In quiet moments just like these
I feel as if the time stands still.

My heart is filled with gratitude.
For all the beauty of this earth.
Oh, God, when I am calm within,
I hear You softly speak to me
In words that touch and lift my soul.

SUNSET AT THE OCEAN

At dusk, the sun retracts her radiant rays.
She slowly dips into the restless ocean.
A dark, deserted shore behind, she leaves,
And colored vapor over breaking waves.

MOONSET, SUNRISE

Moonset, Sunrise
Greet the new day
Bells ring, birds sing.
I gladly awake.

Moonset, Sunrise
Color white clouds
And dreaming hills.
Lake vapors rise.

Moonset, Sunrise
Another day
To care and share
Our woes and joys.

Moonset, Sunrise
Give us a chance
To spread peace
And goodwill on earth.

MONOLOGUE OF RAIN

A ball of fire drew me from the sphere.
In streams, I descended to the arid earth
To cool the crust and clear the muggy air.
I filled the oceans, the rivers, and the lakes.

My fingers touched the first form of life
Deep in the sighing sea, then in the sky.
My silver threads wove forests everywhere,
And strew vivid flowers in their hair.

I adorn the valleys and fertile fields.
Then, run through rivers back to the mother sea.
The sunshine lifts me with the restless wind.
We soar together to do each task we find.

Thunder and lightning herald my arrival.
A rainbow spans the sky when I depart.
I reign in fury and dance with the savage squall;
Yet cheer and comfort an aching hand and heart.

REQUEST FOR RAIN

The drab brown hills lift up their crests
And beg the sky for rain.

The pregnant clouds obey their plea,
And fill their empty crags.

The mountain clothes festively
In lace of vibrant green.

Then celebrates the newborn life
With gratitude and glee.

SUNRISE

The sun is lifting in her grandeur,

Out of the dark and dreary night,

The earth, and with a kiss so tender

Awakens all creation. And light

Reveals the beauty of the land,

God fashioned with His skillful hand.

A ROSE OF BEAUTY

What a poetry of beauty is just a single rose.
She lives up to her duty as queen of flowers grows.

LOOKING THROUGH THE WINDOW

At dawn, I'm looking through my kitchen window.
There they sit on the sill, lined up in a row
My little beggars, waiting for me to throw
Seeds and tasty morsels in the snow.

PAUSE

I pause just for a moment, Dear,
To let my tired body rest
From all the tedious household chores,
So I may start renewed with cheer
My work. I like to do my best
And end each day without remorse.

FALL

Winds are shifting.
Leaves are drifting.
Birds are flying South.

Golden Splendor
Does fall render.
Fruits fall from the trees.

MY FAVORITE TIME OF YEAR

I like winter, spring, and summer cheer;
But fall is my favorite time of the year,
When days stay warm and nights turn cold.
And stalks rustle in the field of gold;
Their blades die gracefully and bend
In gentle motion till the end.

ODE TO A SNOWFLAKE

The snowflakes softly cover
The vast and barren land.

Where did you snowflake come from
That fell upon my hand?

Were you a tear of sorrow,
Or a tear of happiness?

Where will you be tomorrow?
Where will your journey end?

FOG

The fog
Obscures
And dulls the beauty of the day.

The shadow
Will depart.
Soon, the mist will roll away.

The sun
Will shine
Create another radiant day.

Doubts
Depress
And take the joy of life away.

But love
And patience
Burn the Phantom Fog away.

Peace
And gladness
Will again return to stay.

STARS ON THE SEA

The sun splashed many stars
Upon the wavelets of the sea.

Their fleeting beauty sparkled
Just long enough for me to see.

A GLORIOUS DAY

When darkness giveth birth to light,
And gently kisses awake creation,
Early birds flutter in flight
And twitter songs of adoration.
I lift my heart to God and pray
And thank Him for this glorious day.

EVENING

Quietly, the evening came
Like a magician in a golden cloak.
He removed the earth's flame,
And twinkling vapors rose above a rock.

THE PATH OF LIFE

Our paths in life are never smooth.
They have their curves and ups and downs.
It matters not how somber grows
The valley where sorrow roams.

When God is our companion,
We're bound to reach the mountaintop.
In His divine dominion,
God's love will always lift us up.

WINDSTORM

The wind ebbs and swells like a raging sea,
Then grows to a roaring storm.
Jolts trees
Back and forth.
Down to earth
Crash all barren branches.
Weak rooftops tear off from the ranches.

KEEP ON GOING AHEAD

I keep on going ahead,
If I am caught in a raging sea,
And waves seem to swallow my rocking ship.

I can not stop or flee from the Sea
I must steer into the wind my ship,
And keep on going ahead.
Until I conquer tempest and fear
And anchor safely on the pier.

MORNING FOG AT THE SHORE

The distant bluffs
Were wrapped in vapor shrouds.
Just nearby rocks
Had not yet vanished from my sight.

The birds looked for the hidden isles.
I did not hear their songs or cries
Nor motors of the fishermen.
They dared not go to the sea this morn.

And then, at last,
The horizon turned bright.
A disk of light
Rose higher in the East.

Through mist, light beacons pierced,
And spanned a band across the bay.
The dense fog could not halt the sun
From brightening my dreary day.

The vapor vanished.
Familiar surroundings emerged.
The fog turned to clouds,
And rose to the vaulted sky.

A SONG IN THE FIRE

"Why, oh Lord, you send me trials and sorrow?
And let the darkness cloud my joyful heart?"

"Be still, my child, and do not fret for tomorrow.
I'll send you comfort. From you I won't depart.

Be still; you'll hear the sweet, melodic tune
The fire releases from the burning wood.
It once has been a living tree. At noon
The sunlight flecked the tender leaves that glowed.

Birds twittered merrily at dawn and dusk
Their tender trills of joy on his lush branches.
As he grew old, fulfilled his budding task.
He sealed in rings their sweet cadences.

Now, the flaming tongues of fire set free
The imprisoned song, the forgotten melody."

"Oh Lord, You lead me through adversity,
So I can sing a song in the fire to THEE."

RAINBOW AT SUNSET

The sun descends behind the hills and clouds,
And paints two rainbow arches on their shrouds.
A multi-colored band on the sea she lays.
While diving birds break the painted rays with their sprays.

Sailboats cut the colored ribbon of light
As they over the glossy surface glide.
I watch the ever-changing shades of a cloud
Turn purple, pink, then orange, red, and gold.

My clouds reflect the Maker's image and light.
I, too, create some rainbows of delight.
They are bridges to God and global brothers,
So I can share life's depth and beauty with others.

THUNDERSTORM AT SUNRISE

The air was heavy as honey at dawn.
Sun rays could not penetrate
The sticky atmosphere,
Until a thousand flaming swords
Slashed the pregnant clouds.
Torrents of rain
Gushed down to the arid land.
Applauding did the thunder.

NOTHING BUT ASHES

Oh, my God!
Nothing but ashes surround me?
Time passed,
Rain fell.
A flower grew
Beneath two oaks.
They survived the fire
To shade from heat
And shield from storms the flower.

The flower grew
More precious with each day.
And other plants
Did notice it
And humbly bowed
In admiration
To oaks and flower,
Whose bond and joy
Flourished by the hour.

"What happened?" I asked.
"Where have the ashes gone,
That did surround me?"
I mixed through my toil
The ashes with soil
And added some love.
Then, God from above
Did bless the two
And made them prosper and grow.

A SONG OF THE WIND

Today, the wind is in a merry mood.
He gently touches branches of the trees
Who are the strings of his grand forest harp.
He sings and plays his joyful melodies
Among the pines in valleys and on hills.

When he is angry, he lets go his fury.
He plucks and pulls on ev'ry forest cord
Releasing roars and thunders in a hurry.
It quakes and shakes. The weak limbs bend and break.
Even the ground can feel his savage force.

After he displayed his mighty powers,
He softly sings some awesome melodies,
That stir the joyful hearts of lovers
Who dream of bliss and lasting happiness.
They beg the wind to grant their heart's desire.

DANCING WITH THE WIND

Today, the wind plays an exciting tune.
As sea birds gather for their dance at dawn.
Ten pelicans first enter the stage and begin
To undulate above the waves each wing.

A seagull solos high above the cliff
While a flock of vultures glide to catch the drift.
Two scissor tails pierce through the air and bend
And turn to the tune of the whistling wind.

The sunlight slithers through the broken cloud
And foaming waves against the rock applaud.
The palm trees bow and sway in reverence
While watching the birds with the wind today dance.

LOVE

LOVE IS A SONG

Love is a song that never needs to end.
It has the sweetest melody to lend.

The beautiful love of newlyweds only is
A prologue of a grander loving phase.

After sharing years of joy and sorrow
Their love grows deeper; then, tomorrow

Will reflect God's endless love divine,
And be selfless, giving, and sublime.

Their hearts will overflow with melodies,
Lasting here and till eternities.

Love is a song that never needs to end;
It has the sweetest melody to lend.

THE SONG OF GOD'S LOVE

A triumphant song soars
Through the atmosphere each day.
Ancient trees sing
Of life and of eternity.
Sunshine slithers slowly
Through the moving branches
And stirs the hungry heart
With soothing melodies. Then drenches
The spirit with God's Love.

My thoughts leap on wings of faith
To God, my Father in Heaven
Who fills my soul with joy and peace.

OUR MOTHER'S LOVE

You seldom said, "I love you" to each child.
I wonder why your lips were sealed?
Yet every day, you prayed for us anew.
You toiled day-long in every way you knew.

But most of all, you taught us right from wrong,
 A sound foundation to last lifelong.
You shielded us from danger, hunger, and pain.
Your lips never uttered a complaint.

For many years, you raised alone your brood,
And still found time to help the neighborhood.
You ruled your roost with discipline and care,
But never lost your faith in great despair.

We all were blessed that you expressed in deeds,
Your love, by meeting all our daily needs.
The memories of you will linger on,
Until you'll meet in heaven one by one.

FIRST MEETING

The day began like any other day
 Yet it held within its strife
A precious secret to change my life:
By meeting my future spouse on the way

Going down to the laboratory.
He stopped with a friendly greeting,
And a glance that kindled a meeting
Of hearts beginning a love story.

A SONG IN MY HEART

I greet each day with a song in my heart.
May it joy and happiness to you impart.

I shall sing to the sun; she invites me to play.
I shall sing to the moon, for he lights my way.

I shall sing to the birds, the wind, and the sea,
And to you, my love's melody.

I greet each day with a song in my heart.
May it joy and happiness to you impart.

LOVE'S CRADLE

Our hearts became the cradle
Of our newborn babe
Called "Love".

MEDOLDY OF LOVE

Our souls embraced.
Our hearts composed a melody of love.
And through our pulses echoed
A rapid rhapsody of fire.

LOVE'S LONGING

With the birth of each new day,
My heart was longing just to stay
Each precious moment close to you,

To look into your gleaming eyes,
And hear you whisper in my ears,
The sweet expression: "I love you!"

A BOUQUET OF FLOWERS

Just a bouquet of flowers
You picked and to me brought.
Endearing me in your thought,
While I was not with you.

AWAY ON A TRIP

The midnight hour passed.
You're thousands of miles away
Suspended in the sky
Past the Milky Way.

The droning of the plane
Breaks the atmosphere.
Removed from care and pain
You fly to a distant land.

My thoughts fly with you
Across the star-lit sky,
And travel where you go
Till safely you return

OH, DARLING, HOW I MISS YOU

Oh darling, how I miss you,
When you have gone away.
I love you, and I need you,
Each moment, night, and day.

Oh darling, how I miss you,
When you fly far away.
I yearn for your embraces,
Your loving words and kisses.

Oh darling, how I miss you,
When you are far away.
Restlessly, I wait and pray,
"Darling, rush home today."

YOU MADE MY DREAMS COME TRUE

You made so many dreams come true,
When you at our first meeting,
Kindled in me the spark of love,
Whose sacred fire spread and grew
Transforming thus, my very being,
By tasting ecstasy of love.

You gave me so much more than I desired,
You bought for me a lovely home,
Showed me exciting places of the world,
Music and art you treasured and inspired

Me to paint pictures and write poetry.
We viewed life as a vital work of art.

The most precious gift to me:
Is your love so freely expressed.
Without love, life would lose its zest
It would become drab and dreary.
I shall always grateful be,
That love so richly us has blessed.

TEN YEARS AGO

It seems like yesterday, Dear One,
You made your vow come true,
And took me for your wedded wife
To love and cherish me for life.

We set up our country home,
Quite far away from town.
We planted trees and bushes,
And rested when the tasks were done.

We traveled to many countries,
Australia, New Zealand, Asia, Hawaii.
Our lives we filled with memories,
We'll always treasure just you and I.

We shared much joy, but also sorrow
In all the years that quickly passed.
We hope and pray tomorrow,
We'll always be as richly blessed.

EVENING STROLL AT THE LAKE

The weary sun has made a set in gold.
The stars, which are the poetry of the sky,
Adorn the heavens and spread their silver light.
Over the cold and calming waves. The moon
Shimmers and seagulls fly. Their piercing cry
Breaks the stillness of the quiet night.

The breeze hushes to let silence speak.
A chord, in harmony with what we feel,
Is touched within us, and our hearts reply.

I LOVE YOU

I love you!

What great secrets
Do these three hold?

What magic, spoken,
Do they unfold.

It is the sweetest
Story ever told.

YOU DEPARTED

You departed without a goodbye,
And left my broken heart to sigh:
"Why, why have you gone away?
Where are you traveling today?"

Each time the telephone did ring,
I longed to hear your voice.
I hoped, mail men would a letter bring,
To make my aching heart rejoice.

GOING BOATING

It was a sunny summer day,
Just perfect to go boating.
Waves begged to carry us away,
And soon we were departing.

A circle drew the horizon,
Around two lover's hearts,
Beating in blissful accord
With water, wind, and sun.

We talked about so many a thing.
And then again, let silence reign.
The first kiss, a zealous embrace
Deep emotions of love expressed.

STROLLING THROUGH
THE COUNTRYSIDE

We're strolling through the countryside,
Early one Sunday morning
Over green rolling meadows.

Violets bloom along the wayside.
Buttercups are adorning
Fields dotted with cloud shadows.

The breeze combs through the branches.

Birds are chirping in the trees,
While hungry horses graze near ranches.

Bewitched by being in love and
The beauty of nature in springtime,
We're walking happily, hand in hand.

MY HEART IS HEAVY

My heart is heavy
To see you sad.

I won't be happy,
Until you are glad.

FALLING IN LOVE

My hands are fumbling through my work
My heart is beating at a faster pace,
While my soul attempts to capture
The image of my beloved's face.

REFLECTION AND LIFE

DOING OR BEING

Life is filled with things to do.
I plan the work, then rest and go.
Build a career, social positions,
Earn fame and acquire possessions.

Yet, when I stop, reflect, and ponder
There must be more to life, I wonder.
God created men for being
And not only for working or doing.

What matters in my life,
To build through toil and endless strife
A noble character, a heart
To serve others, fulfill God's part.

Life is not just meant to be
A list of tasks, but choosing free
To do God's will, obey and pray
And be His better child each day.

A NEW MASTERPIECE

Lord, this brand new day, a gift from Thee
Is like an empty canvas to be filled
With noble thoughts and good activities
Pleasing Thee and helping others.

Take my patience, kindness, thoughtfulness,
To add more depth and brightness to my art
Splash some shades of sadness here and there
 Creating a harmonious picture.

Then, I spread warm rays of love and joy
To give the painting character and warmth.
God, pour over it Thy holy spirit
So it may glow in iridescent splendor.

We frame in gratitude the canvas,
To delight Thee and others.
Lord, help me each new day,
To create a Masterpiece for Thee.

WHAT IS MATURITY

It is a godly, noble goal for sure,
To mature and always remain pure.
Maturity is more than gaining knowledge, years,
It's choosing what one thinks, does, and hears.
It knows when to listen and when to speak.
Respects the strong, the gentle, and the weak.
Forgiving persons who offend anew,
And saying, I am sorry when it's due.
When I keep my promise and my word,
Trust and honor will be my reward.
To finish the tasks that I began to do,
Even though it's sacrificial to pursue.
I wisely utilize my goods, my time,
Trust and obey God's word, sublime.
God shows me how to choose the right and best.
So, I and others will be richly blessed.

By loving God, myself, my brothers
I demonstrate God's grace to others.
It is a godly, noble goal for sure,
To mature and always remain pure.

LISTENING TO MUSIC

While I do my daily task,
I listen to music; I treasure.
It cheers my heart. I could not ask
For any greater pleasure.

How skillful the composers express
Joy in sweetest melodies.
Life's sorrows they do not repress
By writing moving symphonies.

Music, the language of the soul,
You take me on a joyful stroll,
To exotic places. We travel,
Where beauty and delight enthrall.

BOOKS

Such great treasures are given,
To us, in good books, we read.
They stimulate and enlighten
Our imagination and mind.
Unfold to us a holy creed.
From time to time, we find
Alien visions of tomorrow,

Get a glimpse of earthly sorrow
And all the ugliness we dread.
We learn from great Authors
Who share their fantasies and tales.
And keep us often in suspense,
When we get of their world a glimpse.

WRITING POETRY

I am no Dante, Goethe, Shakespeare,
But I am ingenious and free
And humbly, I dare
To write some poetry.
Life carves a story
In each human heart.
The verses I wrote down
Are just a minute part,
Reflecting my creative mind,
So you may inspiration find.

FRIENDSHIPS

Friendships are like the moving tides and more;
The still receding from the busy shore,
Returning with riches of the sea to share.

PRAISE

Praise is sunshine to the spirit.
It cannot blossom without it.

Criticism is a devastating wind,
It withers the human mind.

A PROMISE

We are not promised easy lives;
But strength and comfort for hard strives.

ZEST OF LIFE

When Christ the Lord lives in my humble heart,
He fills with zest the empty chambers.
So to others, I may spread, impart
Exuberance, love's glowing ambers.
I do not see life with my eyes alone;
I see it with my mind, heart, and soul.
I see the many wonders God has done,
And revere the Maker of them all.
Even though, at times, some problems do arise,
I still put on a smile and greet the day
With gratitude, then wait for the demise.
Of gloom and doom. I work and pray,
That joy and zest of life come to stay,
So I can brighten other's dreary days.
I like to be God's joyous testimonial,
And His loving zestimonial.

I WALK ALONE

I walk alone!
And silence speaks
On the gloomy autumn night.

The moon has gone,
Not one star peaks
Through gray and endless clouds.

My heavy heart slows down my feet,
My eyes are pointing to the ground.
My troubled soul sighs,

"Comfort me! Comfort me!
Lord, my companion be,
And I won't walk alone!"

FAITH OR FEAR

Either faith or fear,
And not perchance,
Guide my thoughts and actions,
Good and bad are recompense
For my wise or wrong decisions.

FRIENDS

Friends are like golden sunshine.
They brighten our days,
By showing love and kindness
In many different ways.

GETTING THINGS IN FOCUS

If we get everything in focus,
Life ebbs and flows in harmony.

Each kind word I have spoken,
Unselfish deeds that I have done,

Has lifted and not broken,
Another person's heart and soul.

SPINNING DREAMS

My hands won't rest,
Until they spin
Each lofty dream
Into a noble deed.

GOD'S INSTRUMENT

OH Lord, Thou Ruler of the Firmament
Thanks be to Thee alone,
That I can be Thine instrument
Through whom Thy will be done.

GOD'S WORD IS TRUTH

Nothing is impossible for Thee,
If we believe, trust, and obey.

God's word is truth and evidence.
Revealing history for human plans.
God bade us to obey and trust,
Have faith in Him, forget the past.
God sacrificed His only son to save
The sinner's souls. To them, He gave
Commandments how to live by faith alone,
And worship God and His beloved Son.
God guides and loves us here on earth.
He'll let us reign with him in paradise.
When we to God our lives surrender,
We grasped a fraction of his splendor.
God gave us victory in trials
And filled our humble hearts with love and smiles.
We honor God through words and selfless deeds
And do our best to meet the people's needs.

Nothing is impossible for Thee,
If we believe, trust, and obey.

A BABY'S GIFT

Every baby brings from heaven:
To mother fragments of beauty from paradise.
And to father is wisely given:

A segment of wonder and possibilities.
Babies thrive in their parents' love,
And grow more precious every day
When raised in God's righteous way.

BUILDING A CRADLE FOR MY GRANDCHILD

I am building a cradle with boards, and love
For my grandchild, God's gift from above,
The fragile thought of yesterday,
Will be a radiant reality.

I wonder if it will be a grandson
With a great destiny, but full of fun.
Or shall I be blessed with a granddaughter,
Who will warm my heart with love and laughter?

When God needs great deeds done on earth,
He sends a baby to a humble hearth.
May God bless this grandchild of mine,
So it will be guided by love divine.

TRIBUTE TO FATHERS

Fathers deserve my great respect.
Their energy, love, and devotion
Set our world in motion.
Fathers keep law and order intact.

Their courage builds a Nation,
Big cities, bridges, a college.
Their wisdom and chief knowledge
Grant children a good education

TRIBUTE TO MOTHERS

A special tribute I do pay
To dedicated, loving mothers
Who plant a seed of goodness

Into their children's hearts, then pray,
So later they will grow, mature
And bear some fruit of greatness.

Mothers are the heart and root,
Of the world's foundation.
The quality of motherhood
Can make or break a Nation.

A GODLY WOMAN

A godly woman is a precious treasure
She brings to God and men a wealth of pleasure.

Her quiet spirit, precious in God's sight,
Evokes her husband's love and brings delight

To family and friends. Her inner beauty
Reflects God's grace and Christ's humility.

Her virtues are the handiwork of God,
Who sanctifies her soul directs each thought.

She's tuned to harmonize with heaven's note
And lives by faith for others and for God.

HOME

Not only do I call my home the place of birth,
Where first, my parents held me in their loving arms.
Now, after years have passed, I call my home the Earth,
For I outgrew continents, the cities, and the farms.

God's precious gift of life was given to me
So I can share nature, the planet, and outer space.
I care for others and live in peace and harmony
With God, myself, and people regardless of creed or race.

Until God's final call to leave behind the planet Earth
And part from flesh to set my soul and spirit free,
So I can live forever in the universe,
My final home and my eternal destiny.

SPECIAL MOMENTS SHARED AT SEA

We left the port and slowly cruised
Around the Island of Hawaii.

The sun retrieved her golden rays,
And darkness cloaked the Sea and Isle.

The full moon rose and cast upon
The restless sea a silvery veil.

A distant flame of fire appeared
Up high, and steam clouds on the shore.

We watched together from the bridge.
With Captain Townsend's family

The flames illuminate the clouds,
And change their shapes continuously,

While streams of molten magma gushed
Through miles of hardened lava veins,

Then, plunged into the foaming Sea,
Releasing steam and fire tongues.

We viewed in awe the restless earth
Display her mighty fireworks.

The ship sailed on. We left behind
The Island with its awesome sight.

Yet memories will remain through life,
Of special moments shared at sea.

GOD IS EVERYWHERE

No matter where I go, Oh Lord,
You meet me there,
To shield me with your rod and word,
God, you are everywhere.

FOUR SEASONS OF LIFE

In spring, we delight in physical beauty.
In summer, we do our duty.
We reap our fruits in the fall.
In winter, we lift to God our soul.

STRANGE COMPANIONS

Body and mind
Are strange companions.

At dawn, the body leaps,
The mind can't keep the pace.

At noon, both walk in unison,
Calm, content, like in a daze.

At eventide, the body crawls,
While the spirit overflows.

And the observing soul
Stands by to console.

MAKING SUPRESATE SAUSAGE

Each year, when cold and long days grow,
In our hearts, warm memories glow.
We gather without stir and strife,
To keep Italian tradition alive.

Filberto shops and organizes,
Pina, our taste buds tantalizes.
Her mother is multi interessate
To stuff just right each supresate,

Aldo, Elsa and Hilda cut meat,
Which Dominic grounds coarsely and neat.
Tony turns inside out each gut.
Albert and Adam keep the charcoal hot.

They broil to perfection tender pork slices,
Prepared by Gulio with vinegar and spices.
HM! What an aroma! What taste!
Morsels are washed down with vine in a haste.

We mix and stuff, tie and prick;
Then, hang each sausage on a stick.
They are marked with a colorful zagarelli,
So they will reach the right owner's belly.

We laugh and joke, chat and chant.
Still, play some poker at the end.
And are happy to once more.
Relive sweet memories of before.

YOU BROUGHT DELIGHT TO THE NIGHT

The sunset draped the hills in splendor
I went for a walk and said Hello to a neighbor.

I thought the only thing missing was music.
Just then, a sound filled the air like magic.

You played the organ slowly and right,
And brought delight to a glorious night.

DEATH OF A FLY

A fly walked close to me on my desk.
I could have picked her up, an easy task.

The temptation to kill her was great;
But then I thought I rather watch and wait.

She has a right to live as much as I,
Why should I take this privilege from a fly?

I watched her move aside, slow down her pace.
After a while, she fell flat on her face.

I touched her gently and pushed her a little ahead.
To my amazement, the fly was dead.

Did the fly know her life was about to end?
Did she want to die close to a friend?

DEATH OF A CHIPMUNK

I went outside this morning,
To begin my garden work,
When I saw a chipmunk lying
Near a piece of decayed bark.

I picked him up and took him in
And tried to keep his body warm.
He was so weak, lifeless, and thin.
He had no strength to climb on my arm.

Then, gently, he laid down his head,
And in a moment, he was dead.
No fight, no struggle to survive,
A gentle passing from life to death.

Oh God, death, I can't defy;
Today, You showed me how to die.

PERPETUAL CREATION

I never cease to pause and ponder,
How God continues to create
Each day, a new wise wonder.
The atoms, stars, and universe
Are born to follow their own fate.

He structures minute unseen quarks.
Into a power-patterned force,
So fierce it could stop life on Earth,
Yet He implants in every seed
A life force to perpetuate.

In outer space so vast and far
He shapes from cosmic dust a star.
Birth and death of suns take place
Simultaneously in space.

God elects to share with men
To guard and carry on his plan.
He will guide and lead us right,
If we trust and obey his might.

DECISIONS

We are who and where we are today,
Because of decisions we made yesterday.
All our actions which accumulate
Mold our characters, decide our fate.
May God himself enlighten our mind
Enflame our humble hearts with love so kind,
To point our fellow men to heaven.
And may to us the strength be given
To stand in trials as solid as a rock,
And be a beacon and a building block.

OLD AND NEW WAYS

I like to adhere to certain old ways.
It gives me stability.

I like to change to some new ways.
It gives me flexibility.

IF I THINK WITH MY HEART
AND FEEL WITH MY MIND,
MY ACTIONS
WILL BE WISE AND KIND.

PITY AND JOY

Oh, how I pity city folks
Who live among tall concrete blocks
Who never see a starlit sky?
Or watch a flock of birds fly by.

Each moment I can spend outside,
I'm happy and quite satisfied.
I view the handiwork of God,
And by His splendor, I am awed.

I watch a sunset by the sea;
It clears my mind, inspires me.
I feel the vastness of the Earth,
The grandeur of the Universe.

A little infusion of beauty each day
Takes negative thoughts and emotions away.
 Nature grants many rewards,
And lifts my spirit heaven-wards.

LITTLE BY LITTLE

Little by little, a bird builds its nest.
Brick by brick, a wall is constructed to last.
We build our lives and happiness, indeed,
With patience and persistence, we succeed.
Nothing worthwhile happens overnight,
It takes time to do things well and right.

Bonds and friendships, which we slowly nourish
Extend a lifetime and do richly flourish.
God, our Father, helps us grow in grace
And guides us wisely at His loving pace.
Little by little grows our feeble faith,
Until we see our Savior face to face.

FRUSTRATIONS

Every life is different, yet the same
Experiences we often share and claim.
Heartaches and frustrations come and go.
We question why and what we should do.
When we hurt and feel the mental strain.
Are we crushed or raised to God again?

If we trust His mercy and obey
In time, God will show his perfect way.
He gives us inner peace and strength each day
When we look up, stand firm and pray.
God heals our hurts, forgives, restores our faith,
He shows us daily love and eternal grace.

In trials, God reveals his greatness,
And renews our strengths and mental fitness.
We do our best and leave with God the rest,
And with a closer walk with God, we're blessed.
God gives wisdom, patience, and joy to those
Who not their own but His will chose.

THE DAWNING OF A NEW MILLENNIUM

A new millennium dawns. My heart is filled
With hope, expectancy, excitement, wonder.

I witnessed epic changes in every field,
And fictions turn to facts. Yet I ponder:

"When will we excise war and crimes,
And learn the art of being kind and wise?"

Though change and growth are painful oftentimes,
They hold promises and blessings in disguise.

I welcome life with each new challenge
And do surrender to the constant change.

I gather knowledge in the noisy world.
In stillness, heaven's wisdom is revealed.

As life proceeds, I grow. In God I trust,
Who opens worlds uncharted in my mind,

And quenches my relentless search for truth,
In change, He lets me peace and purpose find.

When I align my thoughts, my words, each deed
With the Eternal Source, I do succeed.

I'll find the wonders that I plant within,
Blossom in the new millennium.

A FRIEND LIKE YOU

Oh Lord, without a friend like you,
Who made my heart and soul anew;
I would drown in a sea of tears
From daily stress, sorrows, and fears.

PERSONAL QUOTES

Sorrow stretches the chamber of the heart,
So it will be able to hold more joy.

The anguish of the thornbird
Composes a sweet and cheerful song.

The beauty of nature
Looks brighter after the storm.

The rose leaf must be crushed,
To free the delicate, sweet scent.

Storm clouds pass;
But sun- and starlight
And God's Love
Do remain.

FLOWER OF HONESTY

Flower of honesty,
You became so rare!
What is your destiny?
Will you despair?

Are your ears dumb
To my urgent plea?
I am choking, numb,
Help set me free!

Wait, do not die,
My Master and I
To your rescue fly.
We'll stab the strangling lie.

A CONSCIENCE

A sensitive conscience
That responds to the slightest wrong,
Is like a blade of grass
That quivers in a gentle breeze.

A dull conscience
That is not moved by doing wrong,
Is like a solid trunk of a tree,
That does not bend in the wind quite strong.

CONFINING GOD

Attempting to confine God
Is like trying to fit
The water of an ocean
Into a tiny pond!

FORGIVENESS

I often ask myself, "Why should I bother
To forgive my neighbor, sister, brother,
And not remember hurts, offenses, or a lie,
A person who says behind my back so sly,
Who cheats me or robs me of my earthly good?
Forgive those who are malicious and rude?"

God says, "Yes, forgive yourself and everyone,
As I forgave and sacrificed my loving son,
Who died for you. He paid for sin the highest price,
To save you, He has shed his blood by grace."
Even though forgiving is my private choice,
I do obey and listen to God's divine voice.

I know that judgment only does to God belong,
And choose not to revenge bad deeds, a wrong.
God hates sin yet loves the offender.
I honor God when I to Him surrender.
When I forgive, I live in harmony and peace,
And practice kindness, love, and Christian faith.

A SONG WITHOUT WORDS

Each day, I celebrate the joy of life,
And lift my heart above the mundane strife:
I sing a song without a word or sound
They are tunes of my soul, heaven-bound.

God answers me in a key I understand.
For I feel His peace and love upon me descend.
His joy heals body, mind, the soul, emotions
And wipes away the tears of tribulations.

Under the shade of His wings, I sing for joy,
Just knowing His love and presence is always nigh.
I can sing in a crowd or when I am alone
To keep always with God and nature in tune.

EXPRESSING GOD'S LOVE

I try in thoughts, words, and acts to express
God's love, that it may others comfort and bless.

So souls and creation will reverberate
The joy of life, His grace and glory, so great,

A NOSTALGIC JOURNEY

The wind plays in the palms a soft melodic tune.
Darkness gently drapes the land. Soon,
Stars and the moon brighten the dark firmament.
In houses and streets, shimmer lights, and
Like magic on a nostalgic journey fly my thoughts
Home, where long ago my cradle stood.

My childhood memories I fondly relive once more:
When days greet the sky with a sigh, as before,
I roam through forests, and pick flowers in the fields.
Joy and exuberance my carefree heart fills.
Frogs croak. In the distant swamp wades a stork.
I whistle a happy tune with the skylark.

Soon the lazy summer days grow long and warm.
The fields change to a sea of ripe corn.
Timid deer hide in timber and grass their fawn.
I fish in rivers and swim in the nearby pond.
Before I realize the summer dreams are gone.
And wild geese gather already to fly beyond

The Alps to the sunny South. Snowflakes fall, and
Create a magic and peaceful winter wonderland.
Hi Ho! The sleigh bells ring, we gladly ride to school.
We skate on frozen ponds and ski downhill.
Then build a snowman with a broomstick in his hand,
And throw snowballs at our dear friend.

At night, we sit by candlelight, listen to stories
And watch in the hearth the crackling fires.

Mother tells tales of bygone days and haunting ghosts.
They make us shiver and shudder a lots.
The winter passed. Soon, birds return, the snowbells bloom,
And spring arrives like an elegant groom.

Oh, home of my cradle, which stood in a meadow by forests and fields,
You were my treasured childhood paradise.
Homesick, I send tears to kiss wild flowers awake.
I whisper a prayer and sigh for your sake.
I send my longings to the moon, the evening star:
"Please, greet my homeland, so dear and so far."

WORLD WAR II

EAST PRUSSIA

East Prussia, my beloved homeland,
Sheltered in your lap, my cradle stood.
Spellbound by the beauty of nature,
I spent my childhood years there.
You led me by your gentle hand
Through forests and fields.
On the edge of the lush meadow
I picked a bouquet of flowers for my mother.
Before it was dark, I hurried home.
I enjoyed playing at the nearby pond.
For me, the forest was like a paradise.
What a delight to pick berries,
Nuts and mushrooms
Between spruces and beech trees.
Now, it's just a childhood dream,
Because strangers live in the land,
Where once in seven hundred years,
The honest Prussian and my ancestors
Built by diligent work and knowledge
An exemplary country.
I often ask, my beloved homeland,
Why did such a tragic fate meet you?
Seventy-nine years have already passed
Since foreign power holds you captive.
And melancholy still fills my heart,
When I think of the loss of my homeland.

ESCAPE FROM EAST PRUSSIA

We wrote the year Nineteen-Hundred-Forty-Four.
Germany was engaged for five years in the Second World
War.
A ruthless dictator of Austrian ancestry,
Had ruled with force eleven years in Germany.
Then, we lived next to Poland in East Prussia;
Only sixty miles away from the border of Russia.
Our homestead among hills, forests, and fields stood.
Where mother raised eight children alone, Father had fought
Already two weeks on the Eastern front. As we feared,
The Russian Army launched an attack, battlefield neared.

At Midnight, August 3, a messenger knocked on the door.
"It's Urgent! At nine the next morning, be at the village square!
Don't waste time! The battle looks grim. The Russians are
coming."
Mother Shouted: "Children, hurry! Get up! We're leaving!
George, bring the wagon!
Take oats along.
Emma pack food!
Meta, take clothes!
Richard and Ed
Run to the shed,
Feed the geese,
Hens and Turkeys!
Hilda, dress
Little Horst!"
What about Marta?

"She's too far away, and there is no time or means to reach her.
I hope, she will escape with the family of the teacher."
We rushed, packed, and loaded the wagon from midnight to dawn.
Mother served the last breakfast to three daughters, four sons
In the home she loved, where all her eight children were born.
Then, she took a long look at things she cherished. By grief-torn,
She turned to God. to relieve her pent-up parting pain.
Not knowing if she would ever see her homestead again
Filled her eyes with tears and heart with pain. A cry from Horst,
Kept them from overflowing and called her to go forth.

"Emma, take the rein! Hilda, get on the wagon!
The others will walk till we pass over the hill! Let's go!"
Emma, the oldest, ordered the horses to start moving.
We embarked on a journey whose destiny remained unknown.
Senta, the faithful dog, followed us awhile.
Emma chased her back when we stopped on top of the hill
To look back for a moment and say once more good bye.
Not knowing if forever we would have to break our tie
To our home and birthplace, we all held very dear.
"Children, climb up in an hour; we must reach the village square."

The wagon rolled on through meadows and fields of golden wheat.
We stopped in Wizajny other residents to meet.
Restless, horses pulled the wagons in long rows,
And formed an endless trek. "Westwards, the trek goes!"

Shouted a leader, "Get going, and follow each new order!"
We had to escape from the Russians, who broke through
the Prussian border.
Rapidly, the wagon train set in motion.
We joined six other families. Our group of sev'n
Stayed together till the end. The oldest eighty,
A nine-month-old baby and two wounded soldiers on
furlough.

Twenty-four children to feed and clothe by seven mothers,
And being protected by two soldiers and two fathers.
We drove all day, paused at noon, then stopped for the
night.
We slept in barns or houses, whose owners had taken flight.
At times, we camped in forests under star-studded skies.
Wolves howled. Old people moaned. Children's cries
Kept mothers awake most of the night. But on we must press.
More meager became meals as food supplies grew less.
We found a farm, where we could take a well-deserved rest.
September with an abundance of ripened fruit us blessed.

Three sisters generously shared with us their meager goods,
In exchange, boys and girls worked for shelter and foods.
I got sick. Abscesses grew in all my groins.
Fever rose and threatened my life. No medicines
Or doctors could be found. So mother boiled in water
The sharpest knife, then cut to release the pussy matter.
Puss ran from boils, and from my eyes flowed tears of pain.
My feeble body trembled, while jerking again and again.
After this torture, Emma bandaged each throbbing wound.
My body burned with fever, shivered from chills, then found

Relief in a restless stupor and sleep. Each day dropped
The fever. Wounds healed and closed. The pain stopped.
Aches were forgotten. What fun to be able to walk and run.

Meanwhile, the battlefield came closer. We had to move on.
We packed all our goods, some food and took along a cow.
Tied to the wagon, she trotted along. We had fresh milk now.
Soon, the frost coated streets, when temperatures lowered.
Men spanned poles across the open wagons and covered
With blankets the arches to shield their children from cold
and wind.
From dive bombers, we could no protection find.

We ran to the woods, as planes opened fire and bombs
dropped.
To horses and wagons we returned after the attack had
stopped.
Bullets and bombs had ripped people, horses, and carts
apart,
Pieces were thrown into giant fountains of smoke and dirt.
Some met instant death; their bodies shattered, their brains
Exposed. The badly wounded screamed for deliverance
From excruciating pain and sufferance.
Men carried the wounded on top of the undamaged wagons.
Then put out of misery the injured horses, still neighing.
Children whimpered, mothers trembled from fear, thinking,

With each approaching plane and attack, death was near.
Some people had to walk and leave behind their gear.
On moved the trek around bomb pits, debris, and corpses
Of horses and humans. Autumn ended. Food became sparse.
How lucky to find a deserted farm with a pig in the pen,
And cans of fruits in a cellar. All night, the men
Cut up pig's meat that women quickly prepared and shared.
Children found many toys in an attic they had explored.
Boys took a game of checker and chess. Girls were amazed
To find dolls with pretty porcelain faces and braids.

These treasures helped to ease the children's future fear.
By the end of November, the first snow fell. Winter was near.
We passed through a battlefield, heard machine guns,
And watched the fire go up in smoke among the ruins.
Protected by German soldiers, we escaped unharmed.
Too risky to stop; we drove all night. Mother, alarmed,
Discovered next morning, the food supply was gone,
Which was stored in a milk can tied to the wagon.
Only a sack of flour and two jars of lard remained,
Till we cabbage and turnips from a dirt mound obtained.

For breakfast, Mother cooked dumplings with milk from the
cow.
For supper cabbage or turnips, boiled in water from snow.
Pulling the load through snow drifts, drained the horses'
strength.
Adults stumped through the snow with frozen feet and hands.
Hunger pangs left mothers, children, and men exhausted.
God's grace kept us alive and warm the featherbeds.
Families, wrapped in blankets alone, froze to death.
A cloak of snow became their coffins and their graves.
A mother, kneeling in front of a corps, had lost her child.
She prayed to God to end her grief and dreadful plight.

Health and strength declined. Dark eyes, devoid of spark,
Stared in the gory gloom of winter, that left a mark
On old and young alike. The elders made the decision
To stop and find shelter and get a new food provision.
A Polish lady pitied us, gave us one room,
A kitchen and some food. The cow found a home.
Christmas neared. Though far away from our homestead,
We got together and thought of ways to celebrate.
The girls made stars from paper strips and straw.
The boys decided into the woods for a tree to go.

Mother baked cookies and special bread; what a taste!
The roasted goose, a treasured gift, completed the feast.
This brief respite from war and fear made us forget
The horrible sights, hunger, and cold. We gained some weight.
Adults and youth joined us here for New Year's Eve
To ring in the year, Nineteen-Hundred-Forty-Five.
Our dream, short-lived, ended swiftly. The Russians advanced.
We had to press on. Men repaired wagons, the covers reinforced.
And so we began the most arduous, longest stretch of the trip:
Every day, we struggled to survive the grip
Of winter, frostbites, hunger, disease, pain and fear
Of bullets killing us while piercing through the air.
Thousands met their good or ill fate on the Baltic Sea.
Others, packed in unheated freight trains, tried to flee.
Some walked, pressed by the cold into the arms of death,
Ending living hell and perils with their last breath.
We reached the Northern part of the Weichsel River.
To prevent the enemy from crossing over,
Most Bridges were blasted. Now, we embraced the bitter cold
As a friend who spanned a sheet of ice to hold

People, horses, and wagons. But how to drive safely down,
The steep river bank became our resolute problem.
Men felled trees, trimmed them to the proper size,
Then pushed a pole through the rear wheels, so on the ice
They could not turn. Two men on each end held back the beam
To slow the wagons and prevent them from falling over the rim.

Men had put special studs in the horses' shoes to keep
Them from slipping and sliding down the hill, so steep.
Mothers forming lines and holding children's hands crossed,
The river, praying until all people safely passed.

Each wagon was slowly brought down and across the icy
path.
The arduous climb on the west bank began. Men gave a push
To the wagon, each time, horses tried to pull up the load.
Time after time, horses slid back, drenched in sweat
And foaming. At dusk, all seven had reached the top
unharmed.
Under a chilling sky filled with stars, we camped.
Not all were as lucky as we. Some plunged with their horses
and carts
Down the steep bank to their final rest. Without horses and
goods,
Persons had to continue the strenuous journey on foot,
Nobody knew which fate they met or how far they got.

Winter's fury in January and February slowed down our
pace.
Hunger tormented young and old, and food became scarce.
On straw in stables, sheds, or vacant houses, we slept.
Eight down covers, taken along from freezing us kept.
We welcomed spring much more than any year before:
To see trees bud, flowers bloom, birds soar encore,
Removed winter's gloom and poured joy into hearts again.
Now, we could sit in front of the wagon and watch each town
Pass by. We savored the warmth of sunrays on our cheeks.
Children laughed and listened to the trills of the skylarks.

We arrived at Sophienhof, in Schleswig- Holstein,
And shared a one-bedroom apartment with family Hein.
Now we lived in a house and ate plenty of food.

Mother, content, all thirty-four survived, thanked God
For His grace, and prayed that He keep her children protected
From danger and death by bombs, now towards us directed.
No bunkers or basements to hide. We ran into the woods.
Explosions ripped to pieces the earth. We waited and watched.

Children cried, trembled, and feared the end was near.
Only Mother's comforting hands dried each tear.
The air raids continued during the day, the bombing at night
Until, at last, the end of the war halted the fight.
In Nineteen-Hundred-Forty-Five, the eighth of May,
Germany surrendered! The victors shouted: "Hurray!"
How grateful were refugees who reached the West;
Yet the worst horrors awaited the Germans in the East.
At night, the Russian soldiers came and looked around.
They picked up every woman and older girl they found.

Those who resisted were beaten, tortured, or shot on the spot.
The crying victims had to endure their cruel lot:
Being raped more than once or twice each night;
They were forced into a wedge of no escape:
To die or to endure the savage horrors of rape.
Their emotional hurt haunted them for life.
Some ended their agony by using a knife.
Germans, unprotected by any government,
Were killed, beaten, bore hate or cruel punishment:
Homeowners were robbed, accursed, and driven from their land.

The physically able were forced to labor without a cent.
Men and women endured for years such inhuman lives,
Before they rejoined, debilitated their families or wives.

To the West, the feeble, old and young, were in train wagons
shipped,
Or driven like cattle on foot while being cursed and whipped.
Cold, with little to wear and scanty food provisions
Many died before reaching their destinations.
Millions who resisted this monstrous war machine,
Paid a high price so that freedom could reign.
Why did these innocent people die, and endure such hate,

Got a taste of hell and escaped through its gate?
Because their leader, who forced his way to power by killing
Everyone who opposed him or was not agreeing.
The innocent people paid the price of his lust for glory.
He wrote, with blood, the darkest chapter in history.
Who were the victors or losers of this war in the end?
Every country involved did wealth and lives spend.
War heroes were decorated with monuments and medals
of gold
But the stories of heroic mothers and children are seldom
told.
Their courage, patience, endurance, hard work, love and
faith,

Kept alive, during the war, their kin and troubled countries?
Together with soldiers who returned from war, women rebuilt
The destroyed cities, war-torn land, and their broken spirit.
They restored their country, healing the festering war
wounds.
And love blossomed among ashes and city ruins.
But history, as written, will be forever tainted and marred;
And horror exposed how innocent people were killed and
scarred.
Around the table, mother her seven children gathered.
After thanking God, that he spared their lives, she said:
"Children, let joy come as a balm to each troubled heart.

Live wisely, as if tomorrow you might depart.
Don't harbor hate against persons who harmed us during the war,
Forgive them! It will free you from future despair.
Treasure life, and thank God for His precious gift.
Find a reason to live, and give God and people your best.
We hope and pray, that Leaders of all Nations
Will settle their differences through negotiations.
The innocent always suffer! The price is too high by far.
For blood begets blood, hate begets hate, and war begets war.

But peace begets peace; love begets love. And in the end:
All people are brothers. God wants the best for all mankind."

INSPIRATION

FOLLOW THE GLEAM

Pluck a thistle, plant a flower,
Don't let evil good devour.
Bring joy where you find sorrow.
Give the despaired hope for tomorrow.

Kindle in each unkind heart,
Love divine that won't depart.
Should you meet a doubting mind,
Help a more profound faith to find.

May you be a radiant beam,
And a bridge over a stream,
Who inspires others to dream
And follow the divine gleam.

WORK

Working with your hands alone
Makes you a laborer.
A craftsman you become,
When you use muscle and brain.
If you put into it your heart,
Your work becomes a work of art.

127

HONOR LIFE

Honor life,
And you honor God:
For He is the Creator
Of Life
And all that is good.

LOVE, LIFE, ETERNITY

L ike the sun faithfully does ris**e**
O ffering each new day life and ligh**T**
V ictoriously to planets and every creatur**e**
E volving beauty from her spendo**R**.

L et me be unselfish like the su**N**.
I n loving God, myself, and creation. **I**
F athom God as Giver of life and love tha**T**
E ndures on earth and through eternit**y**.

GOD'S WORD

The Bible is God's written word.
Nature is God's thoughts put into action.
One gives us a better understanding of the other.

PERSONAL QUOTES

The deeper we probe into the finite,
The more we stand in awe before the infinite.

Instead of saying: "God Bless America".
I say: "Let every American be a blessing to his country."

Wild geese flying North
Are a living dispatch of nature

Heralding the arrival of spring.

My hands are working in the soil
And feel the quiver of new life.

Only great minds
Can reach the smallest.

Life is like a cactus pear;
If you do not mind the prick
You get the pear.

OH GOD, MY HEART IS ACHING

Oh God, my heart is aching,
To see a human soul
Torment Thee, Thou Eternal Being,
By making Self, their sole idol.
And disregard Thy saving grace.

Oh God, my heart is throbbing
My soul forgiveness cries,
That in my daily living
I did not emphasize
Enough Thy holy love.

Oh God, my heart is praying:
"Have patience with us all.
Let's never cease proclaiming
Thy grace so wonderful.
For perfect is Thy love!"

DUTY IS CALLING

Your eyes are tearing,
I know you are in pain.
Yet duty is calling,
And you follow again.

When you are grieving,
And agony fills your heart
You are still believing
To complete your part.

It matters not,
If you feel bad or good,
You're selfless in thought
And carry well your lot.

NINE INGREDIENTS OF LOVE

1. **PATIENCE**: "Love suffereth long."
It is serene, the best work rendering,
Endureth everything is understanding.

2. **KINDNESS**: "Love in action."
Making happy by being kind.
Infallible is a loving mind.

3. **GENEROSITY**: "Love envieth not."
It shows to others magnanimity.
And harbors no animosity.

4. **HUMILITY**: "Love is not puffed up."
It seals the lips, forgets good done,
And without boasting carries on.

5. **COURTESY**: "Love does not behave unseemly."
Enacting good manners in little things,
Respect and dignity for others brings.

6. **UNSELFISHNESS**: "Love seeketh not her own."
There is no happiness in only taking;
But in serving others and giving.

7. **GOOD TEMPER**: "Love is not easily provoked."
Bad temper inflicts to others great pain.
It destroys bonds when not kept in rein.

8. **GUIDELESSNESS**: "Love thinketh and does no evil."
It sees the noble in everyone.
Criticism shrivels men.

9. **SINCERITY**: "Love rejoiceth in the truth."
It searches for truth with humble minds,
Does not expose the faults it finds.

HOW DO I LOVE? By practicing daily this sublime art.

WHOM DO I LOVE? To everyone, I must kindness impart.
WHY DO I LOVE? God loved us first, and love begets love.

GROWTH OF MY SOUL

As trees, which grow on cliffs,
Force roots through narrow clefts,
Search for water, food,
To survive and thrive in rugged terrain:

So draws my trusting soul,
When threatened by life's storms,
Strength from within
To triumph over sorrow and trials.

Winds twist the trunks.
And bend the branches.
Strong trees don't break, just shake.
They send more roots between the rocks.

My searching soul seeks
Water of life and wisdom
From deep and boundless wells
And heaven's nectar from the sky.

When I stay linked with the land
And the celestial sphere,
My heart grows kind and still;
While my humble spirit soars.

I ask God for His blessings,
Who knows my every need,
And sends me sunshine,
Storms and rainfalls just in time.

If I follow Him,
My soul will grow and bloom.
Her beauty shall reflect
The lovely, true, and the divine.

THE RISEN SAVIOR

Hallelujah, risen is our Savior!
Nature dresses festively
To greet the risen Savior.
Birds and wind sing lavishly,
A Hallelujah choir.

We felt the sting of death
In the bitter cold of winter,
But now we praise with every breath
The resurrected Savior.

We greet Thee humbly risen Lord,
Ask you to fill with joy our hearts.
We praise Thee for Thy victory
Over death and sin, our enemy.
Hallelujah, risen is our Savior!

LET YOUR LIGHT SHINE

As sunlight puts God's beauty on display
And renews His covenant each day,
So should I, through godly thought and deed
Revere God's world He splendidly made.
Shine, shine, spread God's light, divine.

I brush aside the darkness of the night,
And shield myself with sacred truth and might.
So my life reflects God's heav'nly light,
And reveals His love and divine right.
Shine, shine, reflect God's love, divine.

To persons whom I meet along the way,
God's loving character I portray,
So they will yearn to serve God, too,
Or their faith in Jesus Christ renew.
Shine, shine, spread God's light, divine.

HITHERTO, THE LORD HAS HELPED ME

Hitherto, the Lord has helped me
Through many years of trials to victory.
His loving hand held firmly mine. When
I was feeble, weak, or sick, then
He lifted me upon His wings, and
Gave me health and strength to lend
To others, a helping hand as well.
So, some stretches seemed like hell,
 When Jesus had my sins forgiven,
He would meet my soul in Heav'n,
And bid me share His Father's glory
To forever live God's written story.
God has helped me greatly hitherto.
His love will guide my journey, too.

SORROW

Sorrow, power of God's grace,
Reveals men's character in depth.
God breaks us, then remakes us
To bear much fruit of greatness.
God heals the body, mends the soul,
So we can serve Him better still.
While on a rocky road, we walk
God helps us carry our yoke.
When we triumph over every trial
Peace and joy our hearts refill.

I AM NOT ALONE

When storms of life blow long and hard,
And pain and sorrow break my heart,
My God, my friends and strangers meet
My needs just for each day, indeed.

They calm my troubled mind and peace
Replaces grief and fear. They ease
The heavy load. Their love and care
Do comfort me beyond compare.

With God in charge, I do not fear
He loves me and wipes off each tear.
I know God always does what's best.
My faith grows strong. I'm richly blessed.

I trust my God, have precious friends
Who pray and lend their helping hands.
They lift my spirit when it is down.
I thank my God, I am not alone.

SUMMUM BONUM

Some religions lead us to believe,
Faith is the supreme good of life.
Yet Christ taught us a new and crowning creed,
It never fails and is universal indeed:

"Now abideth faith, hope, and love:

But the greatest of the three is LOVE.
By loving God, men, and creation, you will
Indirectly, all other commandments fulfill.

No matter what creed,
How selfless your deed
How noble your thought,
How much you give,
For others, life leave,
If you have no love,
From the spirit above,
It propheteth you not."

A WISH OF A BLIND PERSON

If I could only see three days:

First, I like to see the faces of friends
And all the people who have been so kind.
To let imprint into my mind
The beauty that reflects their soul.

I let my eyes rest on a baby's face
To catch a vision of their innocence
Unaltered by the conflicts of life,
And absorb their loveliness.

The second day, I would rise with the sun
Intoxicate my eyes with the beauty of nature,
And behold the grand panorama
With all its magnificent colors and light.

I would stroll through the painted forest;
Then, look at the splendor of stars at night.
I would visit an Art Museum
To probe into the soul of men.

The things I touched, now I would see.
The evening I would spend in a theater
To watch the drama of a play
And rhythmic motions of ballet.

The third day, I would like to go and see
The hustle and bustle of a big city;
People in their colorful fashions
And observe their facial expressions.

I would go where the rich and poor dwell
To understand how they work and live.
When darkness descends upon me again,
I realized how much there was left to be seen.

Everything I saw became so dear.
From now on, I shall treasure all my senses,
As if tomorrow they would fail.
But sight brings by far the greatest delight.

TAKING INVENTORY ON
NEW YEAR'S EVE

The year is drawing to a close,
It's time to take an inventory.
I recollect in a reflective pause,
The goals I have achieved already.

Hildegard Bonacker Bruni

How far am I away from hopes
And dreams I set out to attain?
Am I sliding down the slopes,
When it's hard to swim against the stream?

Did I reach a high altitude,
Drink beauty from the well of heaven?
Did I have the fortitude
To learn from my misgiving?

I subtract the minus', add the plus',
Thanks be to God, He richly blessed
My endeavors, Knowing thus,
I set new goals. No time to rest.

I must be persistent, strive for the best,
Commit to God my every quest.
His wisdom guides me from above,
So I may prosper and share His love.

MY SOUL HUNGERS FOR WISDOM

My body can be satisfied with food.

Shelter shields me from the heat and cold.

The world lends beauty for my eyes to see,

Good music fills my ears with melody.

My heart finds comfort in friendship and love:

But my soul hungers for wisdom from above.

A MOONLESS MIDNIGHT SKY

I stand in awe before the splendor of the midnight sky.

I can not comprehend the handiwork of my Creator,

Who fashions stars and sends them spinning through the universe.

He scatters moons and planets in the void of space. They fly,

In perfect patterns through the cosmic sphere, then later

Just vanish from my sight, when sun rays reach the earth.

GOOD SEED

Even in the worst of man
There are good seeds,
Waiting to germinate
Through our kind deeds.

PERSONAL QUOTES

Do anything that makes you happy;
But nothing that makes other people unhappy.

Why should I rush to reach my goal?
When I can take my time
And enjoy the process of achieving.

Trouble:
Is either a stumbling block
Or a stepping stone?
What comfort to know,
The choice is mine.

I am content and blessed,
When I function at my best.

Self and silver obstruct the needs of our neighbors
While selfless love heals the wounds of our brothers.

Words are wings
Carrying a message

From my mind
To your heart.

Only a heart that is soft and filled with love
Will not break,
When the waves of life pound it against the
The rocky shore.

CORNERSTONE

An honest, searching, loving heart
Is the cornerstone of greatness.

OUR HILL

The gate is locked.
And silent is the house.
The warm days left,
Cold autumn winds arrived.
Snow will fall
And lull our hill to sleep.

It's lonely now
Around the empty home.
I'm sad to be
Deprived of loving hugs
And friendly smiles,
Of kind conversations, too.

Soon, we will leave
For sunny Mexico.
Nature will watch

Hildegard Bonacker Bruni

Over our treasured hill.
Till we'll return
In spring, when days are warm.

Now miles away
We live and dream each day.
Of our world,
The glorious paradise.
Until our hearts
Rejoice on our hill again.

SPRING

Spring arrives! Nature renews
To paint the earth with brilliant colors.

She lays green leaves of many hues
On all the trees, weeds, bushes.

And with her most artistic touch
She sprinkles with her brushes

Lovely petals on the plants
In multi-colored splendor,

That even the most artistic hands
Of any human could not render.

Then she throws the birds in place
And many other creatures.

She decorates the earthly face,
With exquisite features.

The Greatest Master views her art,
Infuses life with sublime skill.

Spring fills with rapture now my heart.
Her beauty has no parallel.

COME OUTDOORS

Winds are whistling at my window,
Begging me to come outdoors:
"Look, explore the gifts of nature
And pick violets and daisies,
In the woods and open fields.
I'll renew your joy of living
Through a rendezvous with spring."

FEEDING MY FEATHERED FRIENDS

Feeding my feathered little friends
Always pleasure to me lends.

Cautiously comes the big black crow
And stuffs his beak with bread I throw.

Two daring blue jays dive down quick
And many tasty morsels pick.

Then landed, Mr. Cardinal
To taste a tidbit, I let fall.

And in a hurry grabs a pinch
Of crumbs, a little yellow finch.

After their morning interlude,
They chat and chant their gratitude.

THE RISING SUN

Faint starlight filters through the pale pink clouds
And so did broken stripes of greenish blue.
The sea spreads out a velvet quilt of gold
For newborn sun rays to descend and view

The treasures of the life-filled hills then lay
Over the crest, a gilded filigree crown.
Pelican flocks flew over the tranquil bay
To look for schools of fish, then dove down

To catch their fill. The seagulls pierced the air
To greet the sun and her family of rays
Which climbed upon the craggy cliffs, from where
They began to ascend to outer space.

My joyful heart greeted the dawning day.
To my Creator, I began to pray:
"I thank Thee for the sun, the Planet Earth,
For being part of Thy great Universe."

FAITH

THE HOLY TRIANGLE

If I stand alone,
I am like a pole,
That easily is prone
To stumble and fall.

If I have a friend
Who'll walk with me a mile,
We last a very long spell.
If we embrace God
As our companion,
We form a holy triad,

We add equal portions.
Of love, hope, and faith
To create a holy union,
That stands on a solid foundation.

REFLEXIONS

I am a receiver and transmitter of ideas.
If I tune in to the material world
 And accept their philosophy.
I will reflect the timely and the futile!
If, instead, I receive and obey God's divine word,
I will express and transmit the divine and the eternal.

JOURNEY TO BETHLEHEM

A star was shining very bright
Begging me to follow its light.
I journeyed with the holy gleam
Taking me to Bethlehem.

It stopped at a stable to my surprise,
On a newborn babe, I fixed my eyes
Laying in a manger on hay
In such a poor and humble way.

I was ready to depart.
When I heard a song from heaven
"Unto you, the son of God is given."
I listened with my heart.

I knelt, looked at the child again.
My heart embraced God's only son,
While my soul worshipped and beheld
Christ, the Savior of the world.

GOD'S GREAT LOVE

Oh God, my Heavenly Father,
I cannot comprehend
The greatness of Thy Love;
Your only son You sent
To suffer here on earth.
Now, we are free
To worship Thee,
Eternally.

A SYMPHONY OF LIFE

A song of praise and joy of life
Winds play in treetops high.
My heart echoes from deep within
This rhythmic tune from far and nigh.

The waves splash gently on the shore,
And then retrieve into the sea.
Sometimes they pound, then crash and roar
Restless a raging rhapsody.

The birds and bees, the crickets, too
Sing in festive summer choirs.
Music played by instruments
The pensive human heart inspires.

Yet, in the stillness, you can see
The comets pierce the universe.
Some stars are born, and others die.
Life pulsates everywhere on Earth.

God writes a divine symphony
In every noble human heart
Of life and immortality
And of His perfect love and word.

THE CHARACTER OF JESUS CHRIST

In Judea lived a man called Jesus Christ,
By Pharisees rejected by crowds despised
Yet worshipped by His disciples as son of God.
He preached love to all brotherhood.

He wept with the sinners, and with the poor and the rich, he
broke bread.
With a touch and a prayer, He called back to life the dead.
The lame He bid walk, to the blind he restored their sight.
He blessed children, taught adults what's wrong and what's right.

He had compassion, was humble, wise and just,
A son of God, a human, whom we can trust,
A man of extraordinary beauty.
He met men's needs, yet did His Father's duty.

He blessed His accusers and turned the other cheek.
He forgave sinners who acted cruel and weak.
Nailed on the cross, He suffered our sins and died.
With His last breath, He loved us and cried:

"Father forgive them; they don't know what they have done.
Why hast Thou forsaken Thy only son?"
Yet even death could not defy His love,
He left the tomb and rose to His Father above.

"This is my son, in whom I am well pleased.
Believe in Him, and you will live appeased
On earth and in heaven without ending."
Spoke God's a voice from above descending.

A HEART LIKE HIS

(A Study of King David's Life)

David roamed the fields as a shepherd boy
Tended sheep and obeyed God's laws with joy.

He served and worshipped God with heart and soul.
God blessed and chose him for a distinct role.

God increased his wisdom and strength. Fame grew,
When with a sling, the Giant, Goliath, he slew.

With Jonathan, the son of King Saul, he made
A covenant of friendship; they shared their fate.

David loved Saul's daughter, Michal,
But Saul gave her hand in marriage to Patiel.

Then David married Ahinoam of Jezrael,
And later chose a wife named Abigail.

They raised many sons and attractive daughters few.
As a father, he failed; family scandals did brew.

When evil spirits tortured Saul, the restless King,
David would play the harp and for him sing.

As a warrior, he excelled and slew
The Philistines. Much attention he drew

King Saul departed from God's way,
And evil entered into his heart to stay.

King Saul's thoughts brewed jealousy,
He tried to kill David mercilessly.

To save his life, David fled and hid.
Tormented, he begged for mercy from his God.

When David conquered Israel, Saul died
By his sword. David and the people cried.

David also lost his friend Jonathan.
For Judea and Israel, a new era began.

When David was anointed as their King,
They hoped and prayed he would peace to them bring.

King David's rules were just; he obeyed God's will.
He fought, won many wars, and grew stronger still.

He showed kindness to his friend's son
And compassion for the ordinary men.

One day, when King David missed his duty,
He saw a woman of great beauty.

Temptation and desire were so great,
He stole Bathsheba from her mate.

When he learned she had conceived a child,
He sent her husband to the battlefield.

God punished David for his dreadful sin
By letting prematurely die his baby son.

David fasted, wept, and cried to God,
"Spare the child and take my life instead."

He begged God's forgiveness for his sinful act
And promised God to change and live correct.

God's grace removed the curse from them
And blessed them with a second son,

He named him Solomon, whom the Lord loved.
Once forgiven, he worshipped and praised God.

To see the arc, He wished with all his heart,
And go to Judea after Absolom died by his sword.

Once home, he settled his broken family's affair,
And chose for his throne a just and wise heir.

His son, Solomon, was anointed King,
They built a temple and brought an offering.

All people knelt before the Lord in reverence,
And celebrated their kings' benevolence.

People filled the city's square to raise,
To God, their melodies of gratitude and praise,

Through David's house, God sent his only son,
To bring by grace salvation to all men.

We get a glimpse of the glorious day,
When all knees shall bow in worship and pray,

And greet the King of kings and Lord of Lords,
He will take home His bride and fulfill His words.

What are the vital lessons David taught
Throughout all his life's battles that he fought?

He took us to the heights of praising God's glory,
And to the depths of a sad, sinful story.

 Each psalm he wrote expressed a vivid theme
Of his soul's agony or feelings, sublime.

He awoke in us a deep, profound desire
To seek a **Heart like Christ's** in all we aspire.

I AM NOT ALONE

When storms of life blow long and hard,
And pain and sorrow break my heart,
My God, my friends and strangers meet
My needs just for each day, indeed.

They calm my troubled mind and peace
Replaces grief and fear. They ease
The heavy load. Their love and care
Do comfort me beyond compare.

With God in charge, I do not fear
He loves me and wipes off each tear.
I know God always does what's best.
My faith grows strong. I'm richly blessed.

I trust my God, have precious friends
Who pray and lend their helping hands.
They lift my spirit when it is down.
I thank my God, I am not alone.

HOPE FOR MANKIND

When men from moral values do depart,

And evil seems to rule so many nations,

God wakes again within the people's heart

Nobility through His salvation.

Greatness will dawn within the human mind,

Which comprehends God's revelation.

Mankind will peacefully and justly rule again.

The hour is near for Christ's return as King.

To guide His people and to make them free

From sin and bondage. He'll to believers bring

His kingdom down to earth. Redeemed, they

Will reign with Him in peace and harmony

And see the glory of divinity.

They'll worship Him as King of Kings

And Lord of Lords eternally.

TABLE OF CONTENTS

LOVE

REFLECTION AND LIFE

WORLD WAR II

INSPIRATION

FAITH

ABOUT THE AUTHOR

BIOGRAPHY OF HILDEGARD BONACKER BRUNI

Hildegard was born in East Prussia
Near the Kaiser's hunting ground.
In World War II she escaped from Prussia.
In West Germany, a home she found.

She received her former Education
As a Doctor's Assistant in Medicine.
She left behind her German nation.
And became an American Citizen.

To be a poet and study art.
This dream she nourished in her heart.
At the Academy of Art, she gathered knowledge,
Took creative writing at Harper College.

Dr. Aldo Bruni, she later married.
His Clinic for many years she managed.
She wrote a collection of poems
For her husband's tenth Anniversary.

The International Society of Poetry,
Published and taped several poems of hers.
They chose her once as poet of the year.
She improves her writing in every way.

Her poems and paintings are not art alone,
Nor merely a rendering of words and nature
But a mystic marriage of the two
To honor her Creator and delight you.

A Professor from the UCLA
Had this about her work to say:
"The richness of color, harmonious display
Her inner joy and beauty portray."

TO HILDEGARD

Tahoe in the High Sierras
Is a place of Beauty rare.
Mountains, lakes and valleys
Join with Nature everywhere.
And to make the Picture perfect
Bruni's Pictures bring surcease.
With her great creative Talents
The results: a Masterpiece

Keep on painting Gentle Bruni
Art is solace to the Soul,
Art may be the One Salvation
That in the End will make us Whole.

Do not hesitate or falter,
Let not Duty interfere,
Paint on with wild Abandon,
For we know you have no Peer.